FR. DOMINIC IGNATIUS

St. Silouan the Athonite: A Beacon of Holiness in the Modern World

Discovering the Timeless Wisdom of an Orthodox Saint for Today's Spiritual Journey

Contents

Preface

In a world where noise drowns out the whispers of the soul, where the pursuit of material success often leaves behind the echoes of our deepest spiritual longings, the figure of St. Silouan the Athonite emerges as a beacon of quiet wisdom. The modern age, with its relentless pace and constant distractions, presents unique challenges to those seeking a deeper connection with the divine. In the midst of this clamor, many find themselves yearning for something more—something that transcends the superficial and touches the very core of existence.

St. Silouan, a humble monk who lived on the Holy Mountain of Athos, understood this yearning. His life was marked not by grand achievements or worldly accolades, but by a profound inner journey that led him to the heart of spiritual truth. At a time when the world was on the brink of great upheaval, St. Silouan's teachings offered—and still offer—a path to peace, humility, and love.

His wisdom, born out of deep contemplation and intense spiritual struggle, speaks directly to the challenges we face today. In an era where anxiety, loneliness, and spiritual emptiness seem almost epidemic, St. Silouan's message is a balm for the soul. His life, though lived in relative obscurity, resonates across time, offering timeless solutions to the spiritual crises of the modern world.

Through his writings, prayers, and the simple yet profound way he lived his life, St. Silouan invites us to turn inward, to silence the chaos of the external world, and to listen to the still, small voice within. His teachings are not just for the monks of Athos, but for anyone who seeks to navigate the complexities of life with a heart centered on the divine. As we delve into the life and teachings of this remarkable saint, may we find in his example a guiding light that leads us toward a deeper, more meaningful connection with God. In the pages that follow, we will explore not only the historical and spiritual context of St. Silouan's life but also the enduring relevance of his wisdom in our contemporary world.

Introduction

St. Silouan the Athonite stands out among the saints of the Orthodox tradition not merely because of his profound spiritual depth, but because of the extraordinary relevance his life and teachings hold for contemporary readers. In a world where the pace of life accelerates with each passing day, where individuals are often caught between the demands of material success and the yearnings of the spirit, St. Silouan's message offers a strikingly pertinent antidote.

Born into humble circumstances, Silouan's journey to sainthood was not marked by dramatic miracles or public acts of piety. Instead, it was characterized by an intense, inward struggle—a struggle that many today can relate to in their own search for meaning amidst the noise and chaos of modern life. His teachings focus on the essential, timeless truths of humility, love, and the unceasing prayer of the heart. These are not lofty ideals reserved for monks or mystics, but practical guides for anyone seeking a deeper, more authentic spiritual life.

What makes this book unique among the many works on Orthodox saints is its deliberate focus on bridging the gap between the ancient wisdom of the Orthodox tradition and the pressing spiritual needs of today. While many texts provide a historical account or theological analysis of saints' lives, this book seeks to bring St. Silouan's teachings into the context of the 21st century, making them accessible and applicable to a broad audience. It does so by not only recounting his life but by drawing clear connections between his experiences and the universal human experience—offering readers a mirror through which they can see their own spiritual struggles and aspirations reflected.

Moreover, this book delves deeply into the psychological and emotional dimensions of St. Silouan's journey, exploring how his teachings can provide solace and guidance in dealing with issues like anxiety, depression, and the search for purpose—issues that are ever-present in today's society. By highlighting how St. Silouan's life of prayer and repentance can be a model for addressing these challenges, this work stands apart as not just a biography, but a spiritual guidebook for modern times.

In a world where many feel lost or disconnected, St. Silouan's teachings offer a path back to the center, to the stillness where true peace is found. This book aims to make that path visible and accessible, inviting readers to embark on their own journey of transformation, guided by the gentle wisdom of St. Silouan the Athonite.

My Personal Journey

My journey to discovering St. Silouan the Athonite began, as many spiritual journeys do, with a profound sense of searching. It was a time in my life when the pressures of the world seemed insurmountable, and the spiritual practices I had relied on for so long felt inadequate in the face of my growing inner turmoil. Despite a life filled with the blessings of family, career, and community, I found myself grappling with a deep sense of emptiness—a quiet, persistent void that no amount of external success could fill.

I first encountered St. Silouan in a bookshop, tucked away in a corner, almost as if waiting to be found. His image on the cover, serene and contemplative, drew me in. There was something about the way his eyes seemed to gaze beyond the page, a calmness that contrasted sharply with the noise that had come to define my life. I picked up the book, not knowing that within its pages I would find not just a story, but a lifeline.

As I began to read about St. Silouan, I was struck by the simplicity of his life and the depth of his spiritual struggle. Here was a man who, despite living in the isolated sanctity of Mount Athos, wrestled with the very same doubts and fears that plagued my own heart. His early years of monastic life were not marked by immediate peace or spiritual ecstasy, but by a relentless struggle with pride, despair, and the dark night of the soul. Yet, through it all, St. Silouan's unwavering dedication to prayer and his deep humility led him to an encounter with Christ that would forever change his life.

As I delved deeper into his teachings, I found myself returning to his simple yet profound mantra: "Keep your mind in hell, and despair not." It was a paradox that resonated with the core of my own struggles—acknowledging the depths of my despair without letting it consume me. St. Silouan's words became a beacon of hope, guiding me through my own dark nights, reminding me that even in the deepest pits of sorrow, there is always a glimmer of divine light.

The impact of St. Silouan's teachings on my life has been nothing short of transformative. His emphasis on humility, on loving even in the face of suffering, and on the power of unceasing prayer, has slowly but surely begun to reshape my spiritual landscape. I have learned to approach my own struggles not as insurmountable obstacles, but as opportunities to draw closer to God. In moments of doubt, I find solace in his example, knowing that he too walked this difficult path, and emerged from it with a heart full of love and a soul at peace.

Writing this book is, in many ways, a continuation of that journey—a journey I now invite you, dear reader, to join. As we explore the life and teachings of St. Silouan together, I hope that his wisdom will touch your life as profoundly as it has touched mine. May his words inspire you to seek the divine in the midst of your own struggles, and may his example lead you toward the peace that passes all understanding.

Chapter 1: The Early Life of St. Silouan

In the late 19th century, Russia was a land of vast contrasts, where the ancient traditions of Orthodoxy existed side by side with the rapid changes brought on by modernization. It was a time when the Russian Empire, stretching from the Baltic Sea in the west to the Pacific Ocean in the east, was experiencing the tensions of a society caught between the old and the new. While the rural countryside clung to age-old customs and the Orthodox faith, the cities were burgeoning with new industries, ideas, and a restless energy that would soon culminate in the revolutions of the early 20th century.

It was into this world of both spiritual richness and impending upheaval that St. Silouan the Athonite was born. His birthplace, the village of Shovsk in Tambov Governorate, was a typical Russian peasant community, steeped in the rhythms of agricultural life and the deep-rooted piety of the Orthodox Church. Life in Shovsk was simple, and for many, harsh. The villagers' days were dictated by the cycles of the seasons, with the land providing both sustenance and struggle. Yet, amid this simplicity, there was a profound sense of faith, a belief that life's hardships were a path to spiritual growth and salvation.

The Russian Orthodox Church was the heartbeat of these rural communities. It was more than just a place of worship; it was the center of life's most important events—baptisms, weddings, funerals, and feast days. Icons adorned every home, and the sound of church bells marked the passing of time. The faith of the Russian peasantry was one of deep devotion, characterized by frequent prayer, fasting, and an unwavering trust in God's providence. It was in this environment, where the spiritual and the mundane were inseparable, that Silouan (born Simeon Ivanovich Antonov) first encountered the seeds of the faith that would later define his life.

However, this period was also one of great social and political unrest. The serfs had been emancipated only a few decades earlier, in 1861, and the effects of that momentous change were still being felt. While the abolition of serfdom had granted freedom to millions, it also brought economic challenges and dislocation. Many peasants, like Silouan's family, continued to live in poverty, struggling to make ends meet in a rapidly changing world. The rural poor often found themselves at the mercy of larger forces—landowners, government policies, and the unpredictable nature of the Russian climate.

Despite these hardships, or perhaps because of them, the Orthodox faith remained a source of solace and strength. It provided a framework for understanding suffering, not as a meaningless burden, but as a participation in the suffering of Christ. This belief in the redemptive power of suffering would later become a cornerstone of St. Silouan's teachings.

The late 19th century was also a time of spiritual revival within the Russian Orthodox Church. The monastic movement, particularly on Mount Athos, was experiencing a resurgence, drawing men from all walks of life who sought to dedicate themselves entirely to God. This revival was partly a reaction to the secularization and materialism that were increasingly influencing Russian society. For many, the monastic life represented a return to the purity of the early Church, a life of prayer, asceticism, and communion with God.

It was within this complex and dynamic world—rich in spiritual tradition, yet fraught with social and economic challenges—that St.

Silouan was born and raised. His early life was shaped by the deep faith of his family and community, but also by the struggles and uncertainties that were the daily reality for the Russian peasantry. These formative years would lay the foundation for his later spiritual journey, as he sought to reconcile the demands of the world with the call of the divine.

Family and Upbringing

Simeon Ivanovich Antonov, who would later be known as St. Silouan the Athonite, was born into a family where faith was not merely a part of life—it was life itself. The Antonovs were devout Orthodox Christians, living in the small village of Shovsk, nestled in the Tambov Governorate. The family's home was humble, reflecting the simplicity and austerity that marked the lives of Russian peasants at the time. But within its walls, there was a richness of spirit, a deep well of faith that sustained them through the hardships of rural life.

Simeon's father, Ivan, was a man of unwavering piety. Known in the village for his honesty and integrity, he was a living example of the Christian virtues that were the cornerstone of Orthodox teaching. Ivan's days were long, filled with the toil of working the land, but he always found time for prayer and reflection. He was the kind of man who would rise before dawn to say his prayers, his rough hands clasped together in humble supplication. It was said that Ivan never made a decision without first seeking God's guidance, a habit that he instilled in his children from a young age.

Simeon's mother, though quieter in her piety, was no less devout. She was the heart of the home, a woman whose faith was expressed through her care for her family and her neighbors. It was from her that Simeon learned the importance of compassion and charity, virtues that would later become central to his own spiritual teachings. She would often be found at the icon corner in their home, a place of deep reverence where candles burned before the images of Christ and the saints. It was here, at his mother's knee, that Simeon first learned to cross himself, to recite the prayers of the Church, and to feel the presence of the divine in the ordinary moments of life.

The Antonov household was one where religious observance was woven into the fabric of daily life. The family attended church services regularly, participating fully in the liturgical life of the Orthodox Church. Feast days were celebrated with great joy, and fasting periods were observed with solemnity and devotion. Simeon's earliest memories were filled with the scent of incense, the sound of church bells ringing out across the fields, and the sight of flickering candle flames illuminating the faces of the faithful during evening prayers.

From a young age, Simeon displayed a natural inclination toward the spiritual life. He was a quiet and thoughtful child, often found lost in contemplation. Unlike other boys in the village who would spend their days playing and getting into mischief, Simeon seemed to carry within him a sense of the sacred. He was drawn to the stories of the saints, particularly those who had lived lives of great asceticism and prayer. His father would often read to him from the Lives of the Saints, recounting the heroic deeds and deep faith of those who had gone before them. These stories left a profound impression on the young Simeon, stirring within him a desire to pursue a life devoted to God.

But life in the Antonov household was not without its challenges. The family, like many in their village, lived close to the land, dependent on the harvest for their survival. There were years when the crops failed, and the specter of hunger loomed large. Yet, even in these difficult times, the Antonovs' faith never wavered. Simeon's parents taught their children that suffering was a part of life, but it was also a means of drawing closer to God. They believed that through patience, prayer, and trust in divine providence, they would endure whatever trials came their way.

This deep, unwavering faith was the bedrock of Simeon's upbringing. It shaped his character, instilling in him a sense of humility and a profound respect for the spiritual life. As he grew older, Simeon began to feel a strong calling towards monasticism, a path that was not uncommon for young men in his position. The monastic life, with its emphasis on prayer, asceticism, and communion with God, offered a way to live out the faith that had been so deeply ingrained in him from childhood.

In the quiet moments of his early life—whether working alongside his father in the fields, praying with his family at the icon corner, or listening to the tales of the saints—Simeon's soul was being prepared for the great spiritual journey that lay ahead. These formative years in the Antonov household were not just a time of learning the practices of the Orthodox faith; they were a time of deep spiritual formation, laying the foundation for the man who would one day be known as St. Silouan the Athonite.

The Call to Monasticism

Simeon Ivanovich Antonov's journey toward monasticism was not a sudden leap into the unknown, but rather a gradual awakening—a call that grew louder and more insistent with each passing year. The seeds of this calling were planted early in his life, nurtured by the deep faith of his family and the spiritual practices that were as much a part of his daily routine as the work in the fields. But as Simeon grew into young adulthood, the call to a life devoted entirely to God became more than just a distant dream; it became an urgent and undeniable reality.

In his late teens, Simeon began to feel a deep restlessness in his soul, a sense that the life he was living, though good and honest, was not enough to satisfy the deeper longings of his heart. He was a strong, capable young man, known in his village for his physical prowess and hard work. But no amount of labor or earthly achievement could quell the growing desire within him for something more—something that transcended the fleeting pleasures of the world. He found himself increasingly drawn to prayer and solitude, seeking out moments of quiet reflection whenever he could, often retreating to the woods or the banks of the river near his home to commune with God.

Yet, this pull toward the spiritual life was not without its inner struggles. Simeon was a young man, full of vitality and the natural desires that come with youth. He was acutely aware of the temptations that surrounded him—the lure of worldly pleasures, the pursuit of material success, and the pride that can so easily take root in the heart. These temptations were not merely theoretical for Simeon; they were real, tangible forces that he had to confront within himself. He experienced moments of intense spiritual warfare, where the battle between his flesh and spirit raged fiercely. It was during these times that Simeon felt the weight of his own sinfulness most acutely, recognizing the deep need for repentance and purification.

One pivotal moment in Simeon's life came when he found himself deeply moved by the story of a man who had lived a sinful life but experienced a profound conversion through the grace of God. This story resonated with Simeon, as it mirrored his own struggles and the desire for transformation that had taken hold of his heart. The realization that he, too, could turn his life completely over to God filled him with both hope and a sense of urgency. He knew that the path to spiritual freedom would not be easy, but he was determined to pursue it, no matter the cost.

Around this time, Simeon began to hear about the monastic communities on Mount Athos, a place known throughout the Orthodox world as the "Holy Mountain." Mount Athos, with its centuries-old tradition of prayer, asceticism, and spiritual warfare, seemed to Simeon to be the place where he could fully dedicate his life to God. The monks of Athos lived in a way that he deeply admired—a life of solitude, simplicity, and unceasing prayer. For Simeon, the idea of joining such a community was both terrifying and exhilarating. It meant leaving behind everything he had ever known—his family, his village, and the life of a peasant farmer—to embrace a life of poverty, chastity, and obedience.

The decision to leave for Mount Athos was not made lightly. Simeon wrestled with it, aware of the pain it would cause his family, especially his parents, who had always dreamed of him settling down and raising a family of his own. But the call to monasticism was stronger than any earthly attachment. It was as if God Himself was pulling Simeon toward the Holy Mountain, whispering to his heart that this was the path he was meant to walk.

Finally, with his parents' reluctant blessing, Simeon set out for Mount Athos. The journey was long and arduous, taking him far from the familiar fields and forests of his homeland to the rugged, mountainous terrain of Athos. But with each step, Simeon felt a sense of peace and purpose that he had never known before. This was the path of the saints, the narrow way that led to life, and he was determined to follow it to the end.

When Simeon first set foot on the Holy Mountain, he was struck by the palpable sense of holiness that permeated the air. The monasteries, with their ancient stone walls and icons darkened by centuries of prayer, seemed to breathe with the presence of God. The monks, though austere and disciplined, radiated a quiet joy that Simeon had never seen before. It was as if the world had fallen away, and all that remained was the pure, unadulterated pursuit of the divine.

Simeon's early days on Mount Athos were both humbling and challenging. The life of a novice monk was one of hard work, rigorous discipline, and constant prayer. He spent his days laboring in the fields, attending the long church services that filled the monastic schedule, and learning to silence his mind in the stillness of his cell. It was a life that demanded total commitment and a willingness to be broken and remade by God's grace.

But Simeon's inner struggles did not disappear upon entering the monastery. If anything, they intensified. The temptations he had known in the world followed him to Athos, and new spiritual battles arose as he confronted the depths of his own pride, anger, and despair. There were moments when he questioned his decision, when the weight of his sins seemed too great to bear, and the path of monasticism too steep and arduous. Yet, in these moments of doubt and darkness, Simeon found solace in the words of the Church Fathers, in the example of the saints who had walked this path before him, and in the unceasing prayer of the monks who surrounded him.

It was during this time that Simeon began to develop the deep, inner life of prayer that would later define his spiritual teachings. He learned to "keep his mind in hell and despair not," to hold fast to the presence of God even in the face of the most intense spiritual desolation. This period of his life, marked by both great suffering and profound grace, was the crucible in which Simeon was purified and transformed, preparing him

12

for the spiritual heights he would later attain as St. Silouan the Athonite.

In the silence and solitude of Mount Athos, Simeon found what he had been searching for all his life—a life wholly given over to God, free from the distractions and temptations of the world. It was a life of constant struggle, but also of deep peace, as he learned to lay down his own will and submit entirely to the will of God. This was the beginning of Simeon's journey to sainthood, a journey that would take him deeper into the mysteries of the divine than he could have ever imagined.

Chapter 2: The Monastic Journey on Mount Athos

When Simeon first arrived on Mount Athos, the Holy Mountain that had long been a beacon for those seeking a life of prayer and solitude, he was immediately struck by the profound sense of peace that enveloped the peninsula. The ancient monasteries, with their stone walls standing resolute against the elements, seemed to breathe with the prayers of the countless monks who had devoted their lives to God in this sacred place. The air was thick with the scent of incense, and the sounds of the world seemed distant, replaced by the constant, rhythmic chanting of psalms and hymns.

For Simeon, now a novice in the monastic community, the initial days on Mount Athos were a mixture of awe and humility. He had finally arrived at the place he had long dreamed of, a place where the pursuit of holiness was the sole focus, and yet, the reality of monastic life was far more challenging than he had anticipated. The daily routine was rigorous, demanding a level of discipline and dedication that tested the limits of his physical and spiritual endurance.

From the moment he entered the monastery, Simeon was introduced to the unyielding rhythm of monastic life. The day began long before dawn, with the midnight office—hours of prayer and chanting in the darkened church, illuminated only by the flicker of candles. The silence was profound, broken only by the voices of the monks, chanting ancient prayers that had been passed down through the centuries. Simeon, still adjusting to this new way of life, found himself struggling to keep up with the long services, his body weary from the lack of sleep and the unfamiliar demands of the monastic schedule.

But it was not just the physical challenges that tested Simeon; the spiritual tests he encountered were even more formidable. The life of a monk on Mount Athos was not merely about withdrawing from the world—it was about entering into a deep and often painful struggle against the passions, those internal forces that pulled the soul away from God. Simeon found himself confronting temptations he had never imagined, as the quiet of the monastery brought to the surface all the thoughts and desires that had lain dormant in his heart.

Pride, anger, and despair became his constant companions, as he battled to subdue his own will and submit entirely to the will of God. There were moments when the darkness seemed overwhelming, when the weight of his own sinfulness pressed down on him, and he questioned whether he was truly called to this life. The solitude of his cell, meant to be a place of prayer and communion with God, often became a battleground, where the forces of good and evil seemed to wage war over his soul.

Simeon's struggles were compounded by the strictness of the monastic discipline. The monks of Mount Athos lived lives of extreme asceticism, denying themselves even the smallest comforts in their pursuit of spiritual perfection. Food was simple and sparse, often consisting of little more than bread and water, and the work was hard, with each monk contributing to the upkeep of the monastery through manual labor. Simeon spent long hours in the fields, his hands roughened by the toil, and his body aching from the constant physical exertion.

Yet, despite the difficulties, Simeon found moments of profound

grace in this life of sacrifice. There were times when the chanting of
the monks seemed to lift his soul to heaven, when the beauty of the
services filled his heart with a joy that transcended the hardships he
faced. He began to experience what the monks referred to as "the peace
that passes all understanding," a deep, abiding sense of God's presence
that sustained him through the darkest hours of his spiritual journey.

One of the greatest challenges Simeon faced during these early days
on Mount Athos was the temptation to despair. As he struggled with his
own shortcomings and the rigors of monastic life, there were moments
when he felt utterly unworthy of the calling he had received. The
spiritual warfare he encountered was intense, and there were times
when the darkness seemed to close in around him, threatening to
extinguish the light of faith that had brought him to the Holy Mountain.

But in these moments of doubt and desolation, Simeon found strength
in the teachings of the Church Fathers, who had themselves walked the
path of monastic struggle. He learned to cling to prayer, even when
it seemed dry and lifeless, trusting that God was working within him,
even when he could not feel His presence. The words of the Psalms
became his refuge, as he poured out his heart to God in the stillness of
his cell, seeking the strength to persevere.

Simeon also found guidance in the elder monks, who had spent
decades on the Holy Mountain, their lives marked by the deep wisdom
that comes from years of prayer and asceticism. These elders, though
strict in their discipline, were also gentle in their counsel, offering words
of encouragement and practical advice to the young novice. They taught
Simeon the importance of humility, of recognizing his own weaknesses
and relying entirely on God's grace to sustain him.

As the weeks turned into months, Simeon began to settle into the
rhythm of monastic life. The challenges remained, but he found himself
growing stronger, both physically and spiritually. The initial sense of
awe that had accompanied his arrival on Mount Athos deepened into a

profound love for this way of life, a life that demanded everything but offered in return the incomparable gift of communion with God.

Through the trials and struggles of these early days, Simeon was being shaped and refined, his soul prepared for the deeper spiritual journey that lay ahead. The challenges he faced on Mount Athos were not merely obstacles to be overcome—they were the means by which God was drawing him closer, teaching him the lessons of humility, perseverance, and total surrender to His will. And it was through this crucible of monastic life that Simeon would ultimately emerge, transformed and ready to take his place among the saints of the Church, as St. Silouan the Athonite.

Spiritual Disciplines

In the early years of his monastic life on Mount Athos, Simeon Ivanovich Antonov, who would later be known as St. Silouan the Athonite, immersed himself in the rigorous spiritual disciplines that were the foundation of the monastic tradition. These practices were not merely routines; they were the means by which Simeon sought to draw closer to God, to purify his soul, and to transform his inner life. Each day was a cycle of prayer, fasting, labor, and contemplation, all aimed at achieving a state of unceasing communion with the Divine.

Prayer as the Heartbeat of Life

Central to Simeon's spiritual practice was the discipline of prayer, which in the monastic tradition was both a communal and a deeply personal endeavor. The monks of Mount Athos adhered to a strict schedule of daily services, beginning with the midnight office and continuing through the day with Matins, the Hours, Vespers, and

Compline. These services were long, sometimes lasting several hours, and were conducted with a solemnity that reflected their importance in the life of the monastery.

For Simeon, these communal prayers were a source of great spiritual nourishment. The chanting of the Psalms, the incense rising like prayers to heaven, and the flickering of candles in the darkened church—all of these elements combined to create an atmosphere where the presence of God was almost tangible. Yet, it was in the quiet of his cell, in the solitude of the night, that Simeon found the most profound moments of prayer. Here, away from the eyes of others, he engaged in what the monks called "the prayer of the heart," a practice that would become the cornerstone of his spiritual life.

The prayer of the heart, also known as the Jesus Prayer, is a simple yet powerful invocation: "Lord Jesus Christ, Son of God, have mercy on me, a sinner." This prayer, repeated continuously, became for Simeon a way of keeping his mind and heart focused on God throughout the day and night. The goal of this practice was to achieve a state of unceasing prayer, where the invocation of Christ's name would be as constant and natural as breathing. This was no easy task; it required discipline, patience, and the willingness to confront the many distractions and temptations that arose from within.

Simeon's dedication to the Jesus Prayer was total. He would spend hours in his cell, sitting or standing with his prayer rope in hand, repeating the prayer with every breath. In the beginning, his mind would often wander, and he would struggle with distractions. But over time, through persistence and the grace of God, the prayer began to sink deeper into his heart, becoming a source of peace and strength amid the challenges of monastic life. It was through this prayer that Simeon learned to keep his mind fixed on God, even in the midst of physical labor and the daily struggles of the monastic routine.

Fasting and Asceticism: The Discipline of the Body
Alongside prayer, fasting was another essential discipline in Simeon's spiritual practice. The monks of Mount Athos observed strict fasts throughout the year, abstaining from meat, dairy, and often even oil and wine on certain days. These fasts were not merely about denying the body but were understood as a way to purify the soul and gain mastery over the passions. By controlling his physical appetites, Simeon sought to cultivate a spirit of humility and self-denial, recognizing that true freedom comes not from indulging in the desires of the flesh but from rising above them.

Simeon's fasting was rigorous, often going beyond the minimum requirements of the monastic rule. He would eat only enough to sustain his strength for the day's labor, avoiding any excess or indulgence. The food in the monastery was simple—bread, vegetables, and occasionally fish—but Simeon took care to approach each meal with gratitude, mindful of the monastic tradition of eating in silence, accompanied by the reading of the lives of the saints or passages from Scripture. For him, fasting was not a burden but a joyful offering to God, a way of participating in the sufferings of Christ and the saints.

Fasting extended beyond food for Simeon; it was a way of life that encompassed all aspects of his being. He practiced silence, guarding his tongue against idle talk and focusing instead on the words of prayer and Scripture. He also disciplined his thoughts, striving to keep his mind free from distractions and sinful inclinations. This inner fasting, or fasting of the mind and heart, was perhaps even more challenging than the physical fasts, requiring constant vigilance and the grace of God to maintain.

Manual Labor: The Sanctification of Work

Monastic life on Mount Athos was not just about prayer and fasting; it also involved hard physical labor. The monks were responsible for maintaining the monastery, cultivating the land, and producing goods that could sustain the community. Simeon embraced this labor with the same zeal he brought to his spiritual disciplines. Whether he was working in the fields, chopping wood, or performing other tasks, he saw his work as an extension of his prayer life—a way of serving God with his hands as well as his heart.

For Simeon, manual labor was not a distraction from prayer but an opportunity to practice the presence of God in all things. He learned to pray while he worked, repeating the Jesus Prayer as he dug in the earth or carried heavy loads. This integration of prayer and work was a vital part of his spiritual discipline, teaching him to find God not just in the quiet of his cell but in the everyday tasks of monastic life. Through his labor, Simeon developed a profound sense of humility, recognizing that every task, no matter how small or mundane, could be offered to God as an act of worship.

Vigilance and Watchfulness: The Battle of the Mind

One of the most challenging aspects of Simeon's spiritual journey was the discipline of vigilance, or nepsis, as it is known in the Orthodox tradition. This practice involved a constant watchfulness over one's thoughts and emotions, a careful guarding of the heart against the subtle temptations that could lead a monk astray. For Simeon, this was a daily battle, requiring not just external discipline but a deep inner awareness.

The monks taught that thoughts, or logismoi, could be like arrows from the enemy, designed to distract the soul from God and lead it into sin. Simeon learned to recognize these thoughts as they arose, whether they were thoughts of pride, anger, lust, or despair, and to counter them with prayer and humility. This inner warfare was intense, especially in the early years, as Simeon struggled to master his own mind and emotions. But it was through this discipline of vigilance that he began to develop the spiritual clarity and discernment that would later define his teachings.

Vigilance also involved a careful observation of his own behavior, ensuring that his actions were in line with the monastic rule and the teachings of the Church. Simeon was diligent in his obedience to his spiritual elders, recognizing that humility and submission were key to overcoming the passions. He sought to root out any trace of pride or self-will, knowing that these were the greatest obstacles to union with God.

Contemplation and the Experience of God's Presence

As Simeon progressed in his spiritual disciplines, he began to experience moments of deep contemplation, where the presence of God became almost palpable. These moments, though often brief, were like glimpses of heaven, filling his soul with a peace and joy that transcended the struggles of daily life. Through his prayer, fasting, labor, and vigilance, Simeon was being prepared for these experiences, which would eventually lead him to the profound spiritual insights that would later define his legacy as St. Silouan.

In these moments of contemplation, Simeon felt a deep connection to the saints who had gone before him, the great monastic fathers who had also walked this path of asceticism and prayer. He found strength in their example, knowing that he was part of a tradition that stretched back to the earliest days of the Church. This sense of continuity, of being part of a great spiritual lineage, gave Simeon the courage to persevere, even in the face of the most intense trials.

These early years of monastic life were a time of profound transformation for Simeon. Through his unwavering dedication to the spiritual disciplines of prayer, fasting, labor, and vigilance, he was slowly being purified, his soul refined in the furnace of asceticism. It was a hard and often painful journey, but one that would ultimately lead him to the heights of spiritual maturity. In the stillness of his cell and the simplicity of his daily tasks, Simeon was drawing closer to God, preparing himself for the greater spiritual revelations that were yet to come.

Theophany and Spiritual Transformation

Simeon's early years on Mount Athos were marked by intense spiritual struggle and rigorous ascetic discipline, yet they were also the prelude to a profound transformation that would forever change the course of his life. It was during this time of inner turmoil and relentless pursuit of God that Simeon experienced a theophany—a direct vision of Christ— that would become the cornerstone of his spiritual life and teachings.

The vision came after a period of particularly intense spiritual warfare. Simeon had been wrestling with despair, a deep, dark force that seemed to invade his very soul. The temptations he faced were relentless, gnawing at his resolve, filling his heart with doubts about his worthiness and his place on the Holy Mountain. He felt as though he were walking through a valley of shadow, with no light to guide his way. The solitude of his cell, which had once been a refuge, now seemed oppressive, and the once-sweet prayer of his heart felt dry and lifeless. The silence, instead of bringing peace, seemed to echo with the whispers of his own inadequacies and fears.

In this state of desolation, Simeon turned more fervently than ever to prayer. He cried out to God from the depths of his despair, begging for mercy, for a sign that he was not abandoned. It was during one of these desperate nights, as he stood alone in his cell, reciting the Jesus Prayer with tears streaming down his face, that the vision occurred.

As he prayed, Simeon felt an overwhelming presence fill the room—a presence so powerful and holy that it was almost unbearable. He fell to his knees, his heart pounding in his chest, as the air around him seemed to shimmer with a light that was not of this world. And then, in the midst of this brilliant light, Simeon saw Him—Christ, standing before him, radiant and full of indescribable love. The vision was not just of Christ as he had seen in icons, but as the living, glorified Savior, resplendent in divine glory.

Simeon could not speak; he could barely breathe. The sight of Christ filled him with both an immense joy and a profound awe. Every fiber of his being trembled before the holiness of the Lord, and yet, he felt an overwhelming sense of peace, as if all the struggles, all the doubts, had melted away in the presence of this divine light. Christ looked at Simeon with eyes full of compassion and love—love so pure and so intense that Simeon's heart felt as though it might burst. In that moment, he understood that he was fully known, fully seen, and yet fully loved by God.

The vision was brief, but its impact was eternal. As quickly as it had come, the light began to fade, and Christ disappeared from his sight. Simeon was left alone in his cell, but he was no longer the same man.

The despair that had once threatened to overwhelm him was gone,
replaced by a deep and abiding sense of peace. He had encountered the
living God, and that encounter had changed everything.

This theophany was not just a personal experience of divine grace; it
became the foundation of Simeon's entire spiritual life and teaching.
From that moment on, his prayer took on a new depth and intensity. He
continued to struggle, as all monks do, but now with a profound sense
of the presence of Christ within him. The Jesus Prayer, which he had
long practiced, became for him a means of maintaining that connection,
of keeping his heart and mind fixed on the vision of Christ that had
been revealed to him.

Simeon's vision also profoundly influenced his understanding of God's
love and mercy. He had seen firsthand the immense love that Christ
has for every soul, a love that is boundless and unconditional. This
understanding became central to his teachings, particularly his emphasis
on the importance of love and humility. He came to see that the true
path to God was not through extraordinary ascetic feats or intellectual
accomplishments, but through a heart that is humble and filled with
love for God and for others.

The vision also deepened Simeon's awareness of the spiritual battle that
every Christian must face. He understood now that the temptations
and trials he had endured were part of the journey, necessary for the
purification of the soul. The vision had shown him that, even in the
midst of darkness and despair, Christ is always present, always ready to
extend His hand in mercy. This knowledge gave Simeon the strength to
persevere, to continue his ascetic labors with renewed vigor, knowing
that every struggle brought him closer to God.

As Simeon continued his life on Mount Athos, the memory of this vision became a wellspring of spiritual strength. It was not something he spoke of often; in fact, he kept it largely to himself for many years. But it shaped everything he did, from his prayers to his interactions with his fellow monks. He became known for his humility, his gentleness, and his deep love for others—qualities that were all rooted in that profound encounter with Christ.

In time, Simeon's spiritual wisdom became apparent to those around him, and he began to be sought out for his guidance and counsel. He was still a simple monk, living a life of prayer and labor, but there was a depth to his spirituality that others recognized and revered. The vision had not only transformed Simeon personally, but it also began to bear fruit in the lives of those who came to him for spiritual direction.

This profound spiritual experience, this vision of Christ, was the turning point in Simeon's life. It marked the beginning of his transformation into St. Silouan the Athonite, a man whose life and teachings would go on to inspire countless others on their own spiritual journeys. His message was simple, yet profound: to love God with all one's heart, to remain humble, and to trust in the boundless mercy of Christ. It was a message that he lived out every day of his life, and one that continues to resonate with those who seek to follow the path of holiness.

Chapter 3: The Teachings and Sayings of St. Silouan

Humility and Love

S t. Silouan the Athonite's teachings on humility and love form the cornerstone of his spiritual legacy, offering profound insights into the path of Christian holiness. These two virtues, so closely intertwined in his thought, were not abstract concepts for St. Silouan; they were the very essence of the Christian life, the foundation upon which a true relationship with God and others must be built. Drawing from his own deep spiritual experiences, St. Silouan articulated a vision of humility and love that continues to inspire and challenge believers today.

Humility: The Gateway to Divine Grace

For St. Silouan, humility was not simply a virtue to be admired—it was an absolute necessity for the soul's journey toward God. He saw humility as the foundation of all other virtues, the fertile soil in which the seeds of love, faith, and repentance could grow. Without humility, St. Silouan taught, it was impossible to truly know God, for humility alone opens the heart to receive divine grace.

St. Silouan's understanding of humility was deeply rooted in his own spiritual struggles. He often spoke of the dangers of pride, which he viewed as the root of all sin and the greatest obstacle to spiritual progress. Pride, in St. Silouan's view, blinds the soul to its own weaknesses and leads it away from God. It is a form of self-deception, a barrier that prevents the soul from experiencing the true light of Christ. In contrast, humility brings a clear-sighted awareness of one's own sinfulness and a deep dependence on God's mercy.

In his writings, St. Silouan frequently emphasized the importance of self-knowledge as the first step toward humility. He encouraged believers to see themselves as they truly are, without illusions or excuses, and to recognize their utter dependence on God. This self-knowledge, however, was not meant to lead to despair, but to a profound sense of God's love and compassion. St. Silouan taught that when we see ourselves clearly and acknowledge our own weaknesses, we become more open to receiving God's grace.

One of St. Silouan's most famous sayings encapsulates his understanding of humility: "Keep your mind in hell, and despair not." This paradoxical statement reflects his belief that true humility involves an honest acknowledgment of the reality of sin and the possibility of eternal separation from God. However, this acknowledgment must be coupled with an unshakeable trust in God's mercy. For St. Silouan, humility was not about self-loathing or despair, but about maintaining a constant awareness of one's need for God's grace and a deep trust in His love.

St. Silouan's humility was also reflected in his relationships with others. He believed that humility was the key to loving others as Christ loved, without judgment or condemnation. He taught that true humility leads to a compassionate and forgiving heart, one that seeks to see others as God sees them—with love and mercy. This was not an easy path, but

St. Silouan believed it was the only path that led to genuine communion
with God and with others.

Love: The Fulfillment of the Law

If humility was the foundation of St. Silouan's teachings, love was the
fulfillment. For St. Silouan, love was not just an emotion or a feeling;
it was the very essence of God's nature and the ultimate goal of the
Christian life. He taught that to love is to know God, for "God is love"
(1 John 4:8), and to live in love is to live in God.

St. Silouan's understanding of love was shaped by his own experience
of God's boundless love during his vision of Christ. This experience
left an indelible mark on him, filling him with a deep desire to love
others with the same selfless, sacrificial love that he had received. He
often spoke of the need to love not only those who are easy to love but
also those who are difficult, even enemies. This, he believed, was the
true test of Christian love—a love that mirrors the love of Christ, who
prayed for those who crucified Him.

In his teachings, St. Silouan emphasized that love must be active
and self-giving. It is not enough to feel love in one's heart; love must
be expressed through actions—through kindness, generosity, and a
willingness to bear the burdens of others. He believed that love is
the highest expression of the Christian life, the fulfillment of all the
commandments. To love God with all one's heart, soul, and mind, and
to love one's neighbor as oneself—this, according to St. Silouan, is the
essence of the Gospel.

St. Silouan also taught that love is inseparable from humility. Without
humility, love can become self-centered or conditional, based on what
we receive in return. True love, however, is selfless and unconditional,
rooted in a humble recognition of our shared humanity and our
dependence on God's grace. St. Silouan often warned against the

dangers of judging others, teaching that judgment is the opposite of love. To judge others, he believed, is to place oneself above them, to forget one's own sinfulness and need for mercy.

One of the most poignant aspects of St. Silouan's teachings on love is his emphasis on loving one's enemies. He understood this commandment of Christ not as an ideal to be admired but as a practical necessity for the Christian life. He taught that to love one's enemies is to participate in the very life of God, who "makes His sun rise on the evil and on the good" (Matthew 5:45). This kind of love requires a heart that is purified by humility, a heart that sees beyond the sins and faults of others to the image of God within them.

St. Silouan's own life was a testament to the power of love. He lived a life of profound compassion, caring for his fellow monks and offering spiritual guidance to all who sought him out. Even in the face of personal suffering and spiritual trials, St. Silouan remained steadfast in his commitment to love, believing that love was the path to union with God.

The Legacy of Humility and Love

St. Silouan's teachings on humility and love have had a lasting impact on the Orthodox Church and on Christian spirituality more broadly. His insights continue to resonate with those who seek to live a life rooted in the Gospel, offering a path to spiritual transformation that is both challenging and deeply rewarding.

In his writings and sayings, St. Silouan offers a vision of the Christian life that is grounded in the realities of human weakness but also filled with the hope of divine grace. He teaches that humility and love are not just ideals to strive for, but living realities that can transform our hearts and bring us into closer communion with God. Through humility, we come to see ourselves and others as God sees us, with love and mercy.

Through love, we fulfill the law of Christ, becoming vessels of His grace
and instruments of His peace.

This teachings of St. Silouan remind us that the path to God is a path
of humility and love—a path that requires us to lay down our pride, to
forgive those who have wronged us, and to love without condition. It
is a path that leads to true freedom and joy, a path that brings us closer
to the heart of God, where we find the fullness of life in His presence.

Prayer and Asceticism

St. Silouan the Athonite's teachings on prayer and asceticism are
profound, offering a pathway to spiritual depth and intimacy with God
that is both challenging and transformative. Central to his guidance is
the famous and enigmatic advice: "Keep your mind in hell and despair
not." This phrase encapsulates much of St. Silouan's understanding of
the spiritual life, where the intense struggle against sin and despair is
met with an equally powerful hope in God's unending mercy. To truly
grasp the meaning of this teaching, one must delve into St. Silouan's
broader understanding of prayer and asceticism and explore how this
seemingly paradoxical counsel can be applied in the life of the believer.

The Role of Prayer in the Spiritual Life

For St. Silouan, prayer was the lifeblood of the soul, the means by
which one communes with God and maintains a constant awareness
of His presence. Prayer was not merely a ritual or a duty but a living
conversation with God, an intimate dialogue that deepened with time
and practice. St. Silouan emphasized that prayer must come from the
heart, from the deepest part of one's being, where true connection with
God occurs. This kind of prayer, often referred to as "the prayer of the

heart," was central to St. Silouan's spiritual practice.

St. Silouan taught that the Jesus Prayer—"Lord Jesus Christ, Son of God, have mercy on me, a sinner"—was a powerful tool for cultivating this inner prayer. He encouraged the faithful to repeat this prayer continually, both in times of solitude and in the midst of daily activities, allowing it to become a constant rhythm in their lives. The repetition of the Jesus Prayer was not about empty words or mechanical recitation; it was about aligning one's entire being with the presence of Christ, invoking His name with reverence and love.

Through this practice, St. Silouan believed that the soul could be purified, the mind could be focused on God, and the heart could be softened to receive His grace. The Jesus Prayer served as both a shield against temptation and a means of drawing closer to God. As the prayer took root in the heart, it would transform the soul, leading to a deeper awareness of God's love and a greater capacity for humility and compassion.

"Keep Your Mind in Hell and Despair Not": A Paradoxical Wisdom

Among St. Silouan's teachings, his advice to "keep your mind in hell and despair not" stands out as both profound and challenging. At first glance, the phrase seems contradictory—how can one think of hell without falling into despair? Yet, for St. Silouan, this advice was a key to spiritual maturity, rooted in his understanding of the constant struggle against sin and the necessity of maintaining hope in God's mercy.

The phrase "keep your mind in hell" refers to a deep awareness of one's own sinfulness and the very real possibility of separation from God. St. Silouan believed that this awareness was crucial for cultivating true humility. By acknowledging the depth of one's sin and the justice of God's judgment, the soul is brought to a place of sincere repentance.

This is not a morbid or obsessive focus on damnation, but rather a sober recognition of the spiritual stakes and a motivation to strive for holiness.

However, St. Silouan was equally clear that this recognition of sin must be accompanied by a firm trust in God's mercy—hence, "despair not." While the mind acknowledges the reality of sin and its consequences, the heart must hold fast to the hope of salvation. For St. Silouan, despair was one of the greatest dangers in the spiritual life, a trap laid by the enemy to lead the soul away from God. Despair suggests that God's mercy is limited, that there is a point beyond which God will not forgive—a lie that St. Silouan vehemently rejected.

In practice, St. Silouan's advice calls the believer to live in a state of humble vigilance, constantly aware of the need for repentance while simultaneously resting in the certainty of God's love. It is a call to balance the fear of God with the joy of His mercy, to approach the spiritual life with both seriousness and hope. This balance prevents the soul from becoming either complacent or overwhelmed, fostering a steady, enduring faith.

Asceticism: The Discipline of the Body and Soul

Prayer and asceticism were inseparable in St. Silouan's spiritual teachings. He understood asceticism not as an end in itself but as a means to an end—the purification of the soul and the deepening of one's relationship with God. The ascetic practices that St. Silouan advocated, such as fasting, vigils, and manual labor, were all designed to help the believer gain mastery over the passions and to create space for God's grace to work within the soul.

Fasting, for instance, was not simply about abstaining from food but about training the body to submit to the spirit. By controlling physical appetites, the monk learned to control the more dangerous passions of pride, anger, and lust. St. Silouan practiced fasting rigorously, yet always with an awareness of its spiritual purpose. He taught that fasting should lead to greater humility and dependence on God, not to pride in one's own efforts.

Similarly, vigils—extended periods of prayer, often late into the night—were a way of focusing the mind and heart entirely on God. These vigils were times of intense spiritual labor, where the monk battled distractions and weariness to maintain communion with God. St. Silouan's own life was marked by such vigils, which he saw as opportunities to draw closer to Christ and to intercede for the world.

St. Silouan also placed great importance on manual labor, seeing it as an extension of prayer and a means of keeping the body engaged while the mind remained in a state of prayer. Whether working in the fields, building, or performing any other task, St. Silouan sought to do everything with a prayerful heart, offering each action to God as a form of worship. This integration of prayer and work reflected his belief that every aspect of life could and should be consecrated to God.

St. Silouan's teachings on prayer and asceticism are not just for monks on Mount Athos; they offer practical guidance for anyone seeking to deepen their spiritual life. The Jesus Prayer, for example, can be practiced by anyone, regardless of their state in life. It serves as a constant reminder of God's presence and a way to center oneself in the midst of daily activities. For those who find themselves overwhelmed by the busyness of modern life, the Jesus Prayer offers a simple yet powerful way to reconnect with God.

The advice to "keep your mind in hell and despair not" can also be applied by anyone facing the reality of their own sinfulness. In moments of temptation or spiritual desolation, this teaching reminds the believer to maintain both humility and hope. It encourages an honest assessment of one's spiritual state while holding fast to the truth of God's infinite mercy.

St. Silouan's approach to asceticism can be adapted to the circumstances of daily life. Fasting, for example, can take many forms—whether it is traditional abstinence from certain foods or simply the practice of self-control in other areas, such as speech, thoughts, or use of time. Vigils may be difficult for those with demanding schedules, but setting aside regular times for prayer and reflection can serve a similar purpose, allowing the soul to rest in God.

Ultimately, this teaching call the believer to a life of continual conversion, a life marked by constant prayer, humility, and love. They remind us that the path to God is one of struggle and surrender, where the soul must learn to navigate the tensions of the spiritual life with both seriousness and joy. In following St. Silouan's example, we find a way to draw closer to God, to live in His presence, and to experience the peace that comes from a heart fully given over to Him.

On the Condition of Humanity

People often find contentment in their limited circumstances until they encounter something greater. A person can be likened to a village rooster living within a small pen, surrounded by a few people and farm animals, content with his ten hens, simply because he knows no other way of life. But an eagle, soaring high above, perceives vast distances with its keen sight, takes in the sounds of the earth, and marvels at its beauty. The eagle, familiar with many lands, seas, rivers, and a variety of creatures, could never be satisfied living confined within a small pen like the rooster.

This analogy applies to spiritual life as well. Someone who has never experienced the grace of the Holy Spirit is like the rooster, unaware of the eagle's expansive flight. Such a person might know God through nature or Scripture, and they may be content with following the law, much like the rooster is content with its simple life. They do not long for more, as they are unaware of what they are missing. However, one who has encountered the Lord through the Holy Spirit finds themselves drawn to pray day and night. The grace of the Holy Spirit nurtures their love for the Lord, and the sweetness of this love enables them to carry the burdens of life with ease. Their soul longs only for the Lord and constantly seeks the grace of the Holy Spirit.

We all endure suffering on this earth and seek freedom, yet few truly understand what freedom is or where it can be found. The Lord grants peace and freedom to those who repent and turn to Him in love. My dear brothers, while there is still time, let us all repent. God awaits our repentance with mercy, and all the saints in heaven do the same. God is love, and the Holy Spirit in the saints is also love. If we ask for forgiveness, the Lord will grant it. When we are absolved of our sins, our souls will be filled with joy and happiness, and the grace of the Holy Spirit will enter our hearts. In that moment, we will recognize that true freedom is found in God and comes from God.

The grace of God does not restrict our freedom; rather, it helps us keep His commandments. Adam lived in grace, and yet his free will was not restricted. Likewise, the angels dwell in the Holy Spirit without their free will being taken away.

The Lord desires that we love one another, for this is the essence of true freedom — love for God and love for our neighbors. This love embodies both freedom and equality. However, equality is not found in earthly titles, and this should not concern our souls. Not everyone can be a king, a prince, a patriarch, or a leader, but regardless of our titles, we can all love and serve God. In the end, this is what truly matters. Those who love God more on earth will be rewarded with greater glory in His Kingdom.

On God's Will

When you find yourself without kind mentors, it's essential to humbly submit to the will of God. In doing so, the Lord will grant you wisdom through His grace, for His love for us is beyond words.

There is great virtue in surrendering to God's will. When your soul is fully devoted to the Lord, it becomes free from distractions, prays with a pure heart, and feels the love of God, even if the body endures suffering. Once the soul has completely yielded to God's will, the Lord Himself begins to guide it. The soul then learns directly from God, rather than through teachers or Scripture. However, it is a rare blessing for the Lord Himself, through the Holy Spirit, to be the direct Teacher of a soul, and only a few who live in accordance with God's will experience this.

Those who are proud often resist living according to God's will, preferring to control their own lives. They fail to realize that without God, man lacks the ability to truly direct his own life. When I lived in the world without knowing the Lord or the Holy Spirit, I was unaware of the depth of His love for us and relied solely on my own abilities. But once I experienced the presence of Our Lord Jesus Christ through the Holy Spirit, my soul surrendered to God. Now, I accept all adversities with the faith that "The Lord watches over me; what have I to fear?" I couldn't live this way before.

The greatest treasure on earth is to know God and to understand, even partially, His will. A soul that has encountered God must submit to His will in everything, living before Him in both fear and love. In love, because God is love. In fear, because the soul should be cautious not to offend God with any evil thought.

How can you tell if you are living according to God's will? There is a clear sign: if you find yourself longing for something, you have not fully submitted to God's will, even if you believe you have. A person who lives in accordance with God's will does not worry about anything.

If they need something, they entrust it to God; if they do not receive it, they remain content as if they had. A soul that is truly submitted to God's will fears nothing—neither storms nor dangers. Whatever happens, it accepts with the thought, "It is God's will." If the body falls ill, the soul believes, "I must need this illness; otherwise, God would not have allowed it." Thus, both body and soul find peace.

When a soul is burdened by doubt, it should turn to the Lord, and He will respond. However, this should be done primarily in times of crisis and confusion; in ordinary circumstances, it is more humble to seek guidance from a spiritual advisor. The Lord has ensured that the Holy Spirit remains on earth, and those in whom the Spirit dwells experience Heaven within their hearts. You might wonder why you do not feel such grace. The reason is that you have not fully submitted to God's will and continue to live according to your own desires.

We must always pray, asking the Lord to guide us in what we should do, and He will not leave us in confusion. Adam failed to ask the Lord about the fruit that Eve brought to him, and as a result, lost Eden. David did not consult the Lord before taking Uriah's wife, leading to the sins of murder and adultery. Similarly, all saints who have sinned did so because they did not seek God's help and spiritual guidance. Saint Seraphim of Sarov once said, "When I spoke from my own understanding, I made mistakes."

If you speak or write about God, pray and ask the Lord for help and guidance, and He will surely assist and teach you. If you find yourself in confusion, bow three times and say, "Merciful Lord, You see that my soul is troubled, and I fear falling into sin; guide me, O Lord." The Lord, who is ever close to you, will certainly lead you. But if you doubt, you will not receive what you ask for. This is why the Lord said to Peter, "Why did you doubt, you of little faith?" (Matthew 14:31) when Peter began to sink into the water. Likewise, the soul that doubts and begins to drown in evil thoughts will falter.

In the end, only the Lord knows all. As for us, no matter who we are, we must pray for God's enlightenment and seek counsel from our spiritual advisors to avoid making mistakes.

On the nature of the Soul

Judging by the Scriptures and the nature of the people around us, it appears we are living in the final days. Yet, as the great Russian saint, Serafim of Sarov, once said, we must strive to maintain our inner peace, for without it, salvation is impossible. During Serafim's lifetime, his prayers helped safeguard Russia. After him came another spiritual giant, Father John of Kronstadt, who also prayed fervently for the people. He would pray, "Lord, I wish that Your peace would dwell in all Your people, whom You love so boundlessly that You gave Your Only Son to save the world."

Even as he prayed continuously for others, Father John managed to keep his inner peace. However, we often lose our peace because we lack love for others. The Holy Apostles and all the saints longed for the salvation of all people, and while they lived among others, they prayed earnestly for them. The Holy Spirit granted them the strength to love everyone. If we do not love our brothers and sisters, we cannot achieve true peace. This is something we all need to reflect upon.

Glory be to the Lord, who has not left us as orphans but has given us the Holy Spirit to remain with us on earth. The Holy Spirit teaches the soul an unspoken love for others and a deep sorrow for those who have lost their way and are descending into darkness. Those who have not acquired the Holy Spirit often do not wish to pray for their enemies.

Consider the example of Saint Paisii the Great, who prayed for his disciple that had renounced Christ. While he was praying, the Lord appeared and said, "Paisii, who are you praying for? He has renounced

Me." But Paisii, filled with sorrow for his disciple, continued to pray. The Lord then said, "Paisii, you have become like Me in your love."

This is how inner peace is preserved, and there is no other way.

If someone prays often and fasts diligently but does not love their enemies, they cannot find peace in their soul. I could not speak this way if the Holy Spirit had not taught me the importance of love.

You should guide your brother gently, with love. Peace is lost when the soul becomes vain, treats a brother with condescension, or judges and instructs another without humility and love. If you indulge excessively or pray half-heartedly, you will lose the peace within your soul.

However, if we cultivate diligent prayer for our enemies and genuine love for them, peace will remain within our souls. But if we harbor hate or judgment toward our brothers and sisters, our minds will become clouded, and we will lose our inner peace, becoming bold before God without reverence.

Those who carry the peace of the Holy Spirit within them bring peace to others as well. Conversely, those who harbor an evil spirit spread that evil to others. A soul that has experienced God desires to keep Him always within, for He enters quietly, brings peace to the soul, and offers a silent assurance of salvation.

On Grace

The Lord calls sinners to repentance, embracing those who turn to Him with open arms due to His immense compassion, humility, and gentleness. He graciously overlooks past transgressions, making the soul fall deeply in love with Him, reminiscent of a bird longing for the vast, green wilderness.

At times, a soul may find itself devoid of the Lord's grace and ponder over its misdeeds. "I will seek His forgiveness," the soul resolves, "hoping

He will restore His grace, for my deepest desire is only for the Lord."
Such is the comforting nature of the Lord's love that once the soul has
tasted it, it yearns for nothing else. Should the grace diminish, the soul
will fervently pray for its return.

Living in the Holy Spirit brings a soul joy, obviating any longing for
heaven since it experiences the Kingdom of God internally. Yet, when
grace departs, the soul yearns for heavenly connection, seeking the Lord
with tearful pleas.

Those unfamiliar with grace cannot comprehend this longing. Many
are preoccupied with worldly affairs, unaware that no earthly pleasure
can substitute for the presence of the Holy Spirit. By withdrawing His
grace, the Lord teaches humility through merciful wisdom, reminding
the soul of His sacrifice on the Cross. The Lord empowers the soul
to combat adversities, though victory is unattainable without divine
assistance, hence the saying, "Ask, and you shall receive." Without
seeking, we deprive ourselves of the Holy Spirit's grace, leaving the soul
disoriented and blind to God's will.

The simplest route to salvation involves obedience, moderation,
refraining from judgment, and purging one's mind and heart of
malicious thoughts. Embrace the belief that all people are inherently
good and dearly loved by God. These virtuous thoughts attract the Holy
Spirit's grace, allowing one to acknowledge, "God is merciful."

The Lord rejoices in witnessing a soul turn to Him in humble
repentance, blessing it with the Holy Spirit's grace. The timeline for
receiving the Holy Spirit varies; some receive it within months, others
years, and some after decades. Yet, retaining grace requires humility,
often lacking among us.

Saint Serafim experienced divine transformation at 27, profoundly
moved by the Holy Spirit's sweetness. However, upon retreating to
solitude and sensing the loss of grace, he spent three years in repentance,
pleading for mercy. Those fortunate to maintain God's grace progress

from strength to strength. Having once lost grace myself, I was later blessed with an even profounder experience of His mercy. Thus, humble your souls fervently, that the Lord may find them worthy of His love and mercy. Remember, mercy is unattainable without love for our adversaries.

On Penitence

Praise be to the Lord for granting us repentance, a gift that ensures salvation for all who embrace it. Those who reject repentance are doomed to despair, evoking deep pity for their plight.

A soul devoid of peace must repent, and the Lord, in His infinite mercy, will forgive its transgressions, restoring peace and joy. The Holy Spirit alone bears witness to this redemption. True repentance manifests when you detest your past sins, signaling divine forgiveness.

Genuine repentance prepares one to endure life's severest trials—be it hunger, destitution, or extreme climates, and afflictions like illness and poverty. The repentant soul focuses solely on divine pursuit, undistracted by worldly concerns, enabling prayer with unclouded intent. Conversely, those attached to material wealth cannot achieve such spiritual clarity. Incomplete repentance, lacking genuine remorse for sinning against God, leads to a death entangled in unresolved passions.

Even in His final moments, Christ exemplified ultimate forgiveness, pleading for His persecutors. Similarly, Archdeacon Stephen interceded for his executioners. To retain divine grace, we too must extend forgiveness to our enemies. Lacking compassion for sinners facing damnation indicates possession by an evil spirit. To rid oneself of this malevolence requires earnest repentance, freeing the soul from spiritual bondage.

On Servants Of God

The Lord entrusts bishops with the leadership of their congregations
and endows them with the grace of the Holy Spirit. Through this
divine grace, they possess the authority to absolve or retain sins, much
like the Apostles whose successors they are. These leaders guide
us toward Christ, teaching repentance and adherence to the Lord's
commandments. They illuminate our paths with God's word, helping
us to truly encounter the Lord, guiding us on the journey to salvation,
and aiding us in attaining the humble spirit of Christ. They gather the
sorrowful and stray sheep of Christ within the church, aiming to bring
peace to their souls through God.

These pastors intercede for us, praying for our salvation. As friends
of Christ, they can petition Him for humility and the Holy Spirit's grace
for the living, forgiveness for the departed, and peace and freedom
for the Church. Their significant efforts and deeds earn them a
profound understanding of the Saints' lives, which they strive to emulate.
Positioned above others, like eagles, they oversee from great heights,
guiding Christ's flock with theological wisdom.

The role of a priest, who serves at Christ's altar, is significant. To insult
a priest is to insult the Holy Spirit that resides within him. Consider
the story of a humble and gentle man walking with his family who
encountered an archpriest in a carriage. As the man reverently bowed,
he witnessed the archpriest blessing him, surrounded by a radiant grace.

If people could perceive the true splendor with which a priest serves,
they would be overwhelmed by the sight; likewise, if priests could see
the heavenly glory in which they stand during services, they would
commit to asceticism to honor the Holy Spirit's grace within them
without fail.

As I pen these lines, my soul rejoices knowing our pastors mirror
the likeness of the Lord Jesus Christ. Yet, even we, the flock, with

our modest share of grace, reflect the Lord's image. This profound mystery is often unrecognized, but as John the Theologian profoundly stated, "Let us be like Him," not only in death but here and now. The Merciful Lord has sent the Holy Spirit to dwell among us, present in our Church. The Holy Spirit resides in our pure pastors and believers' hearts, teaching us spiritual virtues, empowering us to fulfill the Lord's commandments, and setting us on the path of righteousness.

On Pride and Vanity

Beware of two dangerous thoughts. The first tempts you with, "You are a saint," while the second warns, "You will not be saved." Both are deceptions from the enemy, devoid of truth. Instead, remember this: "I am a great sinner, but the Lord is merciful. He loves His children immensely and will forgive my sins." However, do not rely solely on your deeds, no matter how extensive they might be. An ascetic once boasted to me about his frequent bows, believing it guaranteed his forgiveness. Yet, at his life's end, he was consumed with despair. Thus, it is not by our efforts, but through His grace, that we receive mercy. The Lord favors a humble soul, free from hatred and willing to forgive, and to such a soul, He grants forgiveness joyfully.

If you find yourself observing how others live as a measure of your own virtue, it is a sign of pride. Focus on yourself and you will notice that pride breeds malicious thoughts.

Our adversaries, the demons, succumbed to pride and now tempt us to follow their path, offering false praise. If your soul succumbs to this praise, grace will flee until humility is restored. Embrace the humility of Christ throughout your life.

Vainglory can arise from inexperience or pride. The Lord swiftly corrects the former, but those who suffer from pride endure a longer path to humility.

Vainglory also manifests when we consider ourselves wiser or more experienced than others, including our spiritual advisors.

Regarding spiritual phenomena, if you perceive an internal light or vision but lack a concurrent feeling of love for God and neighbor, be skeptical. Humility will cause such illusions to dissipate.

If you receive visions or dreams, scrutinize them carefully. Genuine divine messages are accompanied by clarity and instruction from the Lord. The enemy, however, mixes sweetness with vanity. If a vision induces confusion or fear, it likely stems from the enemy, particularly if the soul feels unworthy. Conversely, a prideful soul, prone to seeking visions, can easily be deceived.

Divine experiences come through the Holy Spirit, not the intellect. Attempting to know God through intellectual pursuits alone is vainglory; God is known through the Holy Spirit.

On Obedience

Why did the Holy Fathers prioritize obedience over fasting and prayer? Because ascetic practices without obedience can lead to vanity. For the novice, following directions precludes pride. Obedience involves relinquishing one's will entirely, yielding a mind unburdened by worldly concerns, enabling pure prayer. An obedient person focuses solely on God and their spiritual guide's counsel, whereas a disobedient one is distracted by worldly matters and critiques of their elders, obstructing their view of God.

Obedience is crucial not only for monks but for all. Even the Lord exemplified obedience. The proud and self-assured cannot harbor grace, thus lacking internal peace. In contrast, the obedient soul welcomes the Holy Spirit's grace, which brings joy and tranquility.

A person touched by even a hint of grace will embrace leadership gladly, knowing that the Lord governs all creation and his personal circumstances, maintaining peace regardless of the situation.

Obedience curbs pride and in exchange, it bestows the capacity for prayer and the grace of the Holy Spirit, surpassing fasting and prayer in its spiritual efficacy.

Had the fallen angels maintained obedience, they would remain in heaven, praising God. Had Adam preserved obedience, humanity would still enjoy Eden. Yet, even now, returning to Eden through repentance is possible. The Lord's love remains abundant, provided we seek humility and love our enemies. Without love for our enemies, true peace is unattainable, even in paradise

Struggle and Despair

St. Silouan the Athonite's teachings on despair and spiritual darkness are among the most profound and practical aspects of his spiritual legacy. His own life was marked by intense struggles with despair, which he often referred to as one of the most dangerous and insidious of all temptations. Yet, through these struggles, St. Silouan developed a deep understanding of how to combat despair, offering guidance that remains incredibly relevant for people in modern times, where feelings of hopelessness and inner darkness are all too common.

The Nature of Despair in St. Silouan's Teachings

Despair, in St. Silouan's view, is a state of spiritual paralysis, a condition where the soul feels utterly abandoned by God and cut off from His grace. It is more than just a feeling of sadness or depression; it is a profound spiritual crisis that can lead to a loss of faith and a turning away from God. Despair often arises when the soul is overwhelmed by

the weight of its own sinfulness or by the trials and sufferings of life. It
is a state where the soul is tempted to believe that there is no hope of
salvation, no possibility of redemption.

St. Silouan understood despair as a weapon used by the enemy to
separate the soul from God. He taught that despair can take many
forms: it can be the result of prolonged spiritual dryness, a reaction to
personal failure, or even the outcome of intense spiritual warfare where
the soul feels under constant attack. Regardless of its source, despair is
always destructive, leading the soul away from the light of Christ and
into a state of spiritual darkness.

Combating Despair: St. Silouan's Spiritual Strategies

St. Silouan's own struggles with despair led him to develop several key
strategies for combating this dangerous temptation. These strategies
are deeply rooted in the Orthodox spiritual tradition but are also
practical and accessible, offering valuable guidance for anyone facing
the challenges of modern life.

1. Cling to Prayer

The first and most important strategy St. Silouan advocated for
combating despair was to cling to prayer, even when it feels dry or
meaningless. He taught that prayer is the lifeline of the soul, the means
by which we maintain our connection to God, even in the darkest of
times. When despair threatens to overwhelm, St. Silouan encouraged
believers to continue praying, even if all they can manage is the simple
Jesus Prayer: "Lord Jesus Christ, Son of God, have mercy on me, a
sinner."

St. Silouan emphasized that the act of praying, even when it feels empty,
is an expression of faith and a rejection of the lie that God has abandoned

46

us. By continuing to pray, the soul affirms its trust in God's mercy, refusing to give in to the despair that seeks to destroy it. St. Silouan knew from his own experience that there would be times when prayer felt like a burden, but he also knew that these were the moments when prayer was most necessary.

2. Embrace Humility

Humility was central to St. Silouan's approach to combating despair. He taught that despair often arises from pride, from an exaggerated sense of one's own importance or from unrealistic expectations of oneself. When these expectations are not met, the soul can fall into despair, believing that it has failed irrevocably.

St. Silouan counseled that humility—acknowledging one's own weaknesses and limitations—is the antidote to this form of despair. He believed that by accepting our human frailty and recognizing our dependence on God's grace, we can protect ourselves from the pride that leads to despair. Humility allows the soul to see itself clearly, not as a failure, but as a beloved child of God who is always in need of His mercy.

3. Trust in God's Mercy

St. Silouan's teaching, "Keep your mind in hell and despair not," encapsulates his understanding of the balance between recognizing our sinfulness and trusting in God's mercy. He taught that while it is important to acknowledge the reality of sin and the possibility of separation from God, it is equally important to hold fast to the belief that God's mercy is greater than any sin.

St. Silouan believed that despair is a lie because it denies the infinite mercy of God. He encouraged believers to constantly remind themselves of God's love, to remember that no matter how deep the darkness, God's light can reach us. This trust in God's mercy is what ultimately allows the soul to overcome despair, for it redirects the focus from one's own failings to the boundless love of God.

4. Seek the Support of the Community

Although St. Silouan lived much of his life in solitude, he understood the importance of community in combating despair. He often sought the counsel of elder monks and spiritual fathers when he was struggling, and he encouraged others to do the same. In the Orthodox tradition, the spiritual father is a guide who can offer wisdom, support, and reassurance in times of spiritual crisis.

St. Silouan taught that the prayers of others can be a powerful aid in overcoming despair. He believed that when we feel too weak to pray for ourselves, we should ask others to pray for us, trusting that God hears the prayers of the community. This sense of being part of a larger spiritual family can provide strength and comfort when we feel most alone.

5. Practice Acts of Love and Compassion

Another of St. Silouan's strategies for combating despair was to engage in acts of love and compassion, even when one feels overwhelmed by darkness. He taught that by focusing on the needs of others, the soul can be lifted out of its own despair. Acts of kindness and service not only benefit those we help but also remind us of our connection to others and to God's love.

St. Silouan believed that love is the most powerful force against despair. When we reach out to others in love, we open ourselves to the grace of God, which can heal our own wounds and dispel the darkness within us. This outward focus, this turning away from self-centered despair toward the needs of others, is a key element in St. Silouan's approach to spiritual healing.

St. Silouan's teachings on despair are profoundly relevant in today's world, where many people struggle with feelings of hopelessness, isolation, and inner darkness. The pressures of modern life, the constant demands for success, and the pervasive sense of existential uncertainty can all contribute to a deep sense of despair. In such a context, St. Silouan's advice offers a path to spiritual resilience and hope.

His emphasis on prayer, humility, and trust in God's mercy provides a framework for dealing with the challenges of modern life. In a world that often promotes self-reliance and individualism, St. Silouan's teachings remind us of the importance of humility and dependence on God. They call us to seek strength not in our own abilities, but in the grace that comes from surrendering to God's will.

Moreover, St. Silouan's focus on community and acts of love is particularly relevant in a time when many people feel disconnected from others. His teachings encourage us to build and maintain strong spiritual communities, where we can find support and encouragement in times of need. They also remind us that by serving others, we can find healing for our own souls.

St. Silouan's approach to despair is not about denying the reality of suffering but about finding hope and meaning in the midst of it. His life and teachings offer a profound example of how to navigate the spiritual darkness that can so easily overwhelm us, showing that through prayer, humility, and love, we can overcome despair and find the light of Christ in even the darkest times.

Chapter 4: St. Silouan's Influence on Contemporary Spirituality

Orthodox Christian Life

St. Silouan the Athonite's teachings have had a profound and lasting impact on modern Orthodox spiritual practices, especially within monastic settings. His emphasis on humility, love, prayer, and the struggle against despair resonates deeply within the Orthodox tradition, where these virtues have always been central. However, St. Silouan's unique spiritual insights and the intensity of his personal experiences have brought a fresh depth and perspective to these timeless practices, influencing not only monks and nuns but also laypeople seeking to live a life rooted in Orthodox spirituality.

Humility as the Foundation of Monastic Life

One of the most significant ways in which St. Silouan's teachings have shaped Orthodox spiritual practices is through his profound understanding of humility. In monastic settings, humility is considered the bedrock of the spiritual life, and St. Silouan's writings offer a deep exploration of what true humility entails. His teachings emphasize that humility is not merely an outward show of modesty but a deep, inner recognition of one's own sinfulness and complete dependence on God.

In modern Orthodox monasteries, St. Silouan's teachings on humility are often reflected in the daily practices of the monks and nuns. For example, the practice of obedience to one's spiritual father or mother is seen as a way of cultivating humility, as it involves surrendering one's own will in order to follow the guidance of another. St. Silouan's life exemplifies this humility, as he consistently sought the advice and blessings of his elders, even as he grew in spiritual stature.

Monastics also embrace humility through the practice of confession, where they openly acknowledge their sins before God and their spiritual father. St. Silouan's teachings on the importance of self-knowledge and the rejection of pride have reinforced the value of regular confession as a means of maintaining spiritual health and growth. His insistence that true humility involves seeing oneself as the greatest of sinners—yet without despair—has become a guiding principle in Orthodox monastic spirituality.

The Jesus Prayer and the Prayer of the Heart

St. Silouan's emphasis on the Jesus Prayer, or the prayer of the heart, has had a profound impact on the way prayer is understood and practiced in modern Orthodox monasticism. The Jesus Prayer—"Lord Jesus Christ, Son of God, have mercy on me, a sinner"—is central to the spiritual life of Orthodox monastics, and St. Silouan's teachings have deepened its significance.

In monastic communities, the Jesus Prayer is often practiced continuously, both during designated times of prayer and throughout the day. St. Silouan's guidance on integrating this prayer into every moment of life has encouraged monks and nuns to make the Jesus Prayer the

constant rhythm of their lives. His experience of the prayer as a means
of keeping one's mind and heart focused on Christ has been embraced
as a model for achieving unceasing prayer, a goal that many monastics
strive for.

St. Silouan's teachings have also influenced the understanding of the
prayer of the heart, where the Jesus Prayer is not merely recited with
the lips but internalized, becoming a continuous, silent dialogue with
God within the heart. This practice is seen as the path to spiritual
illumination and union with God, and St. Silouan's life is often cited as
an example of the transformative power of this prayer.

Combating Despair and Spiritual Warfare

St. Silouan's teachings on the struggle against despair and spiritual
darkness have become integral to the spiritual formation of Orthodox
monastics. His advice to "keep your mind in hell and despair not"
provides a framework for understanding and confronting the spiritual
challenges that arise in the monastic life.

In modern Orthodox monasteries, there is a strong awareness of the
reality of spiritual warfare, where the soul is constantly engaged in
a battle against the passions, temptations, and the forces of evil. St.
Silouan's teachings on this subject have reinforced the importance of
vigilance, or nepsis, where monks and nuns are taught to guard their
thoughts and remain constantly aware of the spiritual dangers that
surround them.

St. Silouan's own struggles with despair, and his ultimate triumph
through trust in God's mercy, have provided a source of hope and
encouragement for those facing similar trials. His teachings have led
to a greater emphasis on the need for humility and perseverance in the

face of spiritual desolation, as well as the importance of seeking the support and guidance of the spiritual community.

Love and Compassion as Expressions of Faith

St. Silouan's teachings on love and compassion have also had a significant influence on modern Orthodox monastic practices. His insistence that love is the fulfillment of the Christian life, and that true love must extend even to one's enemies, has shaped the way monastics understand their vocation.

In many Orthodox monasteries, acts of love and service are seen as essential components of the spiritual life. Monastics are encouraged to practice hospitality, care for the sick, and engage in works of mercy as tangible expressions of their love for God and neighbor. St. Silouan's teachings on the importance of loving others, even in difficult circumstances, have reinforced the idea that the monastic life is not just about personal sanctification but also about bearing the burdens of others and bringing Christ's love into the world.

St. Silouan's life, marked by profound compassion and a deep love for all people, serves as a model for how monastics can live out the Gospel in their daily lives. His teachings encourage a spirit of gentleness, patience, and forgiveness, qualities that are highly valued in Orthodox monastic communities.

Influence on Lay Spirituality

While St. Silouan's teachings have had a profound impact on monastic life, they have also influenced the spirituality of laypeople within the Orthodox Church. His emphasis on humility, prayer, and love resonates with those seeking to live a devout Christian life in the world. Many laypeople have adopted the Jesus Prayer as a regular part of their

spiritual practice, drawing on St. Silouan's guidance to integrate this
prayer into their daily routines.

St. Silouan's teachings on combating despair are also relevant to
laypeople, particularly in a modern world that often fosters anxiety,
isolation, and hopelessness. His advice to trust in God's mercy and to
seek support from the Christian community provides valuable counsel
for those struggling with the challenges of contemporary life.

Moreover, St. Silouan's example of humility and love has inspired
many Orthodox Christians to pursue these virtues in their own lives,
fostering a spirit of compassion and service within the broader Church
community.

Global Impact

St. Silouan the Athonite's influence extends far beyond the boundaries
of Orthodox Christianity, touching the lives of spiritual seekers across
the globe. His teachings, deeply rooted in the Orthodox tradition,
have resonated with people from diverse backgrounds and religious
traditions who are drawn to his profound insights into the human
condition, the nature of God, and the path to spiritual transformation.
St. Silouan's writings, translated into numerous languages, have found a
wide and appreciative audience, making him one of the most influential
spiritual figures of the 20th century.

A Universal Appeal: The Human Struggle and the Search for God

One of the reasons St. Silouan's teachings have had such a global impact is their universal appeal. At the heart of his writings is a deep understanding of the human struggle—the battle with pride, despair, and the search for meaning in a world that often seems indifferent to the soul's deepest longings. St. Silouan's honesty about his own spiritual struggles, his profound humility, and his unwavering faith in God's mercy have made his teachings accessible and relevant to people from all walks of life.

Spiritual seekers from various religious traditions, as well as those who do not adhere to any particular faith, have found in St. Silouan's writings a kindred spirit. His reflections on the nature of prayer, the importance of humility, and the experience of God's love speak to the universal human experience of seeking connection with the divine. In a world where many feel disconnected from traditional religious institutions, St. Silouan's teachings offer a pathway to a deeply personal and transformative spiritual life.

Influence in the West: Christian and Non-Christian Readers

St. Silouan's influence is particularly notable in the Western world, where his writings have been embraced by both Christians and non-Christians alike. Within Christian circles, especially among Catholics, Anglicans, and Protestants, there has been a growing interest in the spiritual wisdom of the Orthodox tradition. St. Silouan's teachings on prayer, particularly the Jesus Prayer, have been adopted by many Western Christians as a powerful tool for deepening their spiritual lives.

In addition to traditional Christians, St. Silouan's writings have attracted the attention of those involved in the broader spiritual and contemplative movements in the West. His emphasis on inner silence, contemplation, and the direct experience of God has resonated with people who are exploring forms of spirituality that transcend institutional boundaries. St. Silouan's teachings on the prayer of the heart, for example, have been compared to the practices of Christian mystics like St. John of the Cross and Teresa of Avila, as well as to certain meditative practices found in Eastern religions.

Moreover, St. Silouan's reflections on the nature of suffering and the human condition have found a receptive audience among those who are grappling with existential questions. His understanding of despair, not as an end but as a gateway to deeper faith, has been particularly impactful for people dealing with issues of depression, anxiety, and the search for meaning in a secular world. St. Silouan's advice to "keep your mind in hell and despair not" has been cited as a powerful antidote to the nihilism and despair that often accompany modern life.

Interfaith Dialogue and Comparative Spirituality

St. Silouan's teachings have also played a role in interfaith dialogue and the study of comparative spirituality. Scholars and spiritual practitioners from various religious traditions have recognized the depth of his insights and have engaged with his writings in the context of exploring common spiritual themes. His teachings on humility, compassion, and the struggle against the ego have been particularly relevant in discussions that seek to find common ground between Christianity and other world religions.

For instance, Buddhist and Hindu practitioners have found parallels between St. Silouan's teachings on the purification of the heart and similar concepts in their own traditions. The emphasis on overcoming the ego, cultivating humility, and practicing unceasing prayer or meditation are themes that resonate across religious boundaries. St.

Silouan's life and teachings are often studied alongside those of other great spiritual figures, such as the Dalai Lama, Mahatma Gandhi, and Thomas Merton, as part of a broader exploration of global spirituality. In addition, St. Silouan's writings have been discussed in the context of Sufism, the mystical branch of Islam, where the emphasis on love, humility, and the direct experience of God echoes many of the themes found in the writings of Sufi saints. His teachings on the universal nature of God's love and the importance of loving one's enemies have been seen as bridging the gap between Christian and Islamic mysticism.

Psychological and Therapeutic Applications

Another area where St. Silouan's influence has extended beyond Orthodox Christianity is in the field of psychology and therapy. His deep understanding of the human psyche, particularly his insights into despair, guilt, and the need for forgiveness, has been increasingly recognized by psychologists and therapists who are interested in the intersection of spirituality and mental health.

St. Silouan's teachings on the destructive nature of pride and the healing power of humility have been applied in therapeutic settings, where clients are encouraged to explore their own vulnerabilities and to cultivate a sense of self-compassion. His emphasis on the need for divine mercy and the importance of forgiveness, both of oneself and others, has been used to help individuals who are struggling with issues of guilt, shame, and reconciliation.

Moreover, the Jesus Prayer, as taught by St. Silouan, has been explored as a form of meditative practice that can help reduce stress, anxiety, and depression. The repetitive nature of the prayer, combined with its focus on divine mercy, has been shown to have calming effects on the mind and to foster a sense of inner peace. St. Silouan's teachings on the integration of prayer into daily life have also influenced the development of mindfulness practices that are now widely used in therapeutic contexts.

Cultural Impact and Popular Media

St. Silouan's influence has also permeated popular culture and media, where his life and teachings have been the subject of books, documentaries, and artistic works. His story, marked by intense spiritual struggle and profound mystical experiences, has captured the imagination of writers, filmmakers, and artists who are drawn to themes of spiritual transformation and the search for God.

Documentaries and films about St. Silouan have introduced his life and teachings to a wider audience, making his story accessible to those who might not otherwise encounter the spiritual richness of the Orthodox tradition. His image, often depicted in icons and religious art, has become a symbol of spiritual endurance and hope, inspiring people from diverse backgrounds to explore his teachings further.

A Saint for All Humanity

St. Silouan the Athonite's teachings have transcended the boundaries of Orthodox Christianity, reaching spiritual seekers worldwide who are drawn to his deep wisdom and spiritual authenticity. His insights into prayer, humility, love, and the struggle against despair offer a universal message that speaks to the deepest needs of the human soul. In a world that is often fragmented and divided, St. Silouan's teachings provide a path to spiritual wholeness and communion with God that is accessible to all.

As his writings continue to be studied and applied by people from diverse religious and cultural backgrounds, St. Silouan's influence will likely grow even further, making him not just a saint of the Orthodox

Church, but a spiritual guide for all humanity. His life and teachings remind us that the search for God is a universal journey, one that transcends the boundaries of tradition and speaks to the heart of every human being.

Chapter 5: St. Silouan and Modern Mental Health

Spiritual Healing

St. Silouan the Athonite's teachings have a profound relevance to modern mental health, particularly in the ways they address issues such as depression, anxiety, and despair. His deep understanding of human suffering and his spiritual strategies for combating inner darkness offer valuable insights for both spiritual and psychological healing. In a world where mental health challenges are increasingly recognized as major concerns, St. Silouan's holistic approach to spiritual and emotional well-being is both timely and timeless.

Understanding Human Suffering

St. Silouan's teachings are rooted in a profound empathy for human suffering. His own experiences with spiritual and psychological anguish—manifested through periods of intense depression and despair—gave him a deep insight into the human condition. He understood that such feelings are not merely disturbances to be suppressed or medicated away but are often expressions of a deeper spiritual and existential struggle.

For St. Silouan, mental anguish often arises from a disconnection from the divine and a loss of hope in God's mercy. His approach to dealing with these issues was fundamentally spiritual: he saw the restoration of one's relationship with God as the ultimate healing for the soul. However, his teachings also offer practical wisdom that can be applied in more secular contexts, making them valuable for addressing mental health issues even outside of a religious framework.

Combatting Depression and Despair

St. Silouan's most famous dictum, "Keep your mind in hell, and despair not," encapsulates his approach to combatting despair. This paradoxical advice encourages an acknowledgment of one's own suffering and sinfulness while simultaneously holding on to hope. This can be particularly effective in dealing with depression, where individuals often feel overwhelmed by a sense of worthlessness and hopelessness.

By encouraging a realistic yet hopeful assessment of one's situation, St. Silouan's approach can help individuals break the cycle of negative thoughts that often characterize depressive states. His insistence on the necessity of hope, grounded in the infinite mercy of God, offers a powerful counter-narrative to the hopelessness that accompanies severe depression.

Anxiety and the Importance of Inner Peace

St. Silouan placed great emphasis on the acquisition of inner peace as a central goal of the spiritual life. He taught that this peace comes from a deep trust in God's providence, which can calm the soul even in the midst of life's trials and anxieties. For modern mental health, this emphasis on peace and trust can translate into practices that help reduce anxiety.

Techniques such as mindfulness and meditation, which have been shown to be effective in reducing anxiety, share similarities with St. Silouan's teachings on prayer and attentiveness to the present moment. His advice to live in a state of continual prayer can be adapted to encourage a state of mindfulness, where one is fully present in the moment and less dominated by anxious thoughts about the past or future.

Spiritual and Psychological Integration

One of the most valuable aspects of St. Silouan's teachings for modern mental health is his model of integrating spiritual and psychological well-being. He recognized that spiritual struggles often manifest as psychological problems and that addressing one's spiritual life can have profound effects on one's mental health.

This holistic approach is increasingly being recognized in the field of mental health, where professionals are beginning to appreciate the role of spiritual and existential factors in psychological well-being. Therapies that integrate spiritual practices, such as meditation or prayer, with more traditional psychological interventions are becoming more common and are supported by a growing body of research.

Practical Applications

St. Silouan the Athonite's teachings, with their deep spiritual insights and practical wisdom, offer valuable guidance for those seeking to improve their spiritual and mental well-being in their daily lives. Here are some practical ways to incorporate his teachings into everyday routines, helping to foster a deeper connection with the divine and a more peaceful state of mind.

1. Integrating the Jesus Prayer into Daily Life

One of the central elements of St. Silouan's practice was the Jesus Prayer: "Lord Jesus Christ, Son of God, have mercy on me, a sinner." This simple, profound prayer can be a powerful tool for maintaining a constant connection with God throughout the day.

- **Morning Routine:** Begin the day with a few minutes of quiet time dedicated to the Jesus Prayer. This sets a spiritual tone for the day ahead and helps center the mind.
- **During the Day:** Use the Jesus Prayer as a way to refocus during daily tasks, especially when feeling stressed or overwhelmed. It can be silently repeated during commutes, breaks, or while doing chores.
- **Evening Reflection:** End the day with a period of reflection, using the Jesus Prayer to review the day's events and one's responses to them, fostering a spirit of repentance and gratitude.

2. Practicing Humility and Self-Reflection

St. Silouan placed great emphasis on humility, which he saw as the foundation of spiritual life. Practicing humility involves a realistic assessment of one's own strengths and weaknesses.

- **Journaling:** Keep a daily or weekly journal to reflect on personal failings and virtues. This practice can help develop self-awareness and humility by confronting one's own imperfections without falling into despair.

- **Service to Others:** Engage regularly in acts of service. Volunteering or simply helping out friends, family, or neighbors can cultivate humility and shift focus from self to others.

3. Combating Despair with Hope

"Keep your mind in hell, and despair not" can be understood as staying aware of one's flaws and the darkness in the world without losing hope in God's mercy.

- **Daily Reminders of Hope:** Create daily reminders of God's mercy and love. This could be through scripture verses placed around the home or office, or setting aside time each day to read spiritual literature that emphasizes divine mercy.
- **Spiritual Counseling:** Regularly engage with a spiritual counselor or a trusted mentor who can provide guidance and encouragement in times of spiritual struggle.

4. Embracing Community Support

St. Silouan acknowledged the importance of community in spiritual life. Engaging with a supportive community can provide encouragement and practical help in times of need.

- **Participate in Community Activities:** Whether it's attending services at a place of worship, joining a study group, or engaging in community service, involvement in a community can enhance spiritual growth and provide crucial support.
- **Virtual Communities:** For those who cannot easily access a physical community, virtual communities, especially those centered around spirituality and mental health, can offer support and

connection.

5. Mindfulness and Meditation

Drawing parallels between St. Silouan's teachings on prayer and modern practices of mindfulness and meditation can be beneficial.

- **Mindfulness Practices:** Incorporate mindfulness techniques into daily routines, such as mindful breathing or walking. These can help cultivate presence and awareness, reducing stress and anxiety.
- **Meditative Prayer:** Dedicate specific times for meditative prayer, focusing deeply on the presence of God, similar to the practice of the Jesus Prayer mentioned earlier.

6. Routine of Fasting and Simplicity

St. Silouan advocated for fasting and a simple lifestyle, which can also benefit mental health by reducing the complications and stressors associated with modern consumerist lifestyles.

- **Regular Fasting:** Implement regular fasting days or periods based on personal health and circumstances. This practice is not only spiritually beneficial but can also improve physical health.
- **Simplify Lifestyle:** Actively work to simplify one's lifestyle. This could involve decluttering physical spaces, reducing unnecessary expenses, or limiting digital consumption, creating more space for spiritual activities.

Chapter 6: The Legacy of St. Silouan

Canonization and Recognition

St. Silouan the Athonite was canonized as a saint by the Ecumenical Patriarchate of Constantinople in 1987, several decades after his death in 1938. This recognition came after a thorough examination of his life, teachings, and the impact he had on others, both during his lifetime and posthumously. The canonization process in the Orthodox Church is both rigorous and deliberate, ensuring that the life of the individual truly embodies the virtues and holiness that the Church seeks to uphold in its saints.

Reasons for Canonization

The reasons behind St. Silouan's canonization are multifaceted, reflecting his profound spiritual legacy, which continued to grow after his death thanks to the dissemination of his writings and teachings by his disciple, Elder Sophrony. Here are some key factors that contributed to his recognition as a saint:

1. **Holiness of Life**: St. Silouan's life on Mount Athos was marked by deep humility, unceasing prayer, and ascetic struggle. His personal

journey from a simple peasant in Russia to a monk on Mount Athos showcased his dedication and obedience to God's will. His life was a testament to the transformative power of divine grace when coupled with human effort and humility.

2. **Depth of Spiritual Insight and Teachings**: St. Silouan's teachings, particularly those on humility, love, prayer, and the spiritual battle against despair, offered a fresh perspective within the Orthodox tradition. His insights, especially his admonition to "keep your mind in hell and despair not," were seen as profound contributions to Orthodox spiritual literature and thought.

3. **Impact and Influence**: Even during his lifetime, St. Silouan was known for his spiritual wisdom and was sought after by many for guidance. After his death, his influence grew significantly through the works of Elder Sophrony, who wrote extensively about him and published his writings. The universal appeal of his teachings, which resonated with people across cultural and denominational boundaries, highlighted his significance as a spiritual guide.

4. **Miracles and Reports of Intercessions**: As with many saints, reports of miracles and answered prayers through St. Silouan's intercession played a role in his canonization. Individuals claimed to have experienced healings and spiritual help after praying for his intercession, which further attested to his continued presence and activity within the life of the Church beyond his earthly life.

5. **Veneration Among the Faithful**: Over the years, a growing number of faithful came to venerate St. Silouan, drawing spiritual strength from his life and words. This widespread veneration and the advocacy of influential Orthodox theologians and clerics were crucial in propelling his case for canonization.

Process of Canonization

The process leading up to St. Silouan's canonization involved meticulous scrutiny of his life and works. This process typically includes the collection and examination of writings by and about the candidate, verification of miracles attributed to his intercession, and a theological evaluation of his teachings. The local synod where the saint lived and served plays a significant role in gathering this evidence, which is then presented to a higher church authority—in this case, the Ecumenical Patriarchate.

Once all evidence is reviewed and deemed to fulfill the criteria for sainthood, a formal declaration is made, officially recognizing the individual as a saint. This recognition not only honors the saint but also holds up his or her life as a model of Christian virtue and holiness for the faithful to emulate.

Commemoration and Devotion

St. Silouan the Athonite is commemorated with deep reverence and devotion in the Orthodox Church, particularly since his canonization in 1987. His feast day, liturgical hymns, and the widespread veneration of his icons reflect his enduring impact on the spiritual life of the faithful. These forms of commemoration not only honor his memory but also serve as means through which the faithful can seek his intercession and aspire to emulate his virtues.

Feast Day

St. Silouan's feast day is celebrated on September 24th, according to the Orthodox liturgical calendar. This day is set aside each year to remember his life, teachings, and spiritual legacy. On this day, special services are held in Orthodox churches around the world, including the Divine Liturgy, where special prayers and hymns dedicated to St. Silouan are chanted. The feast day provides an opportunity for the faithful to reflect on the themes central to St. Silouan's life—humility, prayer, love for God and neighbor, and the enduring struggle against despair.

Liturgical Hymns

The Orthodox tradition of commemorating saints includes the singing of special hymns known as troparia and kontakia, which are composed in honor of the saint's life and spiritual achievements. These hymns for St. Silouan encapsulate key aspects of his spirituality and petition his intercession for the faithful. Here is an example of a troparion for St. Silouan:

"By your prayers, you received Christ as your Master on the path of humility. In your heart, the Holy Spirit witnessed to your salvation. Therefore, all people called to live in hope are glad and celebrate your memory. Holy Father Silouan, pray to Christ God to save our souls."

These hymns are not only theological affirmations but also serve as catechetical tools that teach the faithful about the saint's life and virtues. They are typically sung during the Divine Liturgy and other liturgical services on his feast day and on other appropriate occasions throughout the church year.

Icons

Icons of St. Silouan are venerated in many Orthodox churches and monasteries, particularly in places associated with the Athonite monastic tradition. These icons often depict him as a monk, with a humble and gentle countenance, sometimes holding a scroll inscribed with one of his notable sayings, such as "Keep your mind in hell, and despair not." The veneration of his icon is a way for the faithful to seek his spiritual guidance and intercession. It is common for Orthodox Christians to light candles before these icons as a sign of their prayerful intentions.

Personal Devotions and Pilgrimages

Devotion to St. Silouan has also inspired personal and communal forms of piety. Many faithful undertake pilgrimages to places associated with his life, particularly to the Monastery of St. Panteleimon on Mount Athos, where he lived and is now buried. These pilgrimages are spiritual journeys that seek to draw closer to God through the intercessions of St. Silouan, asking for his guidance in emulating his deep faith and humility.

Additionally, many personal prayer books and spiritual writings include prayers for his intercession, reflecting his influence on individual spiritual lives. Devotees often read passages from his writings, especially those on prayer and humility, as part of their daily spiritual exercises.

Educational Impact

Beyond the liturgical and devotional practices, St. Silouan's impact is also felt in Orthodox education. Seminaries and religious education programs frequently include studies on his life and teachings, using his experiences as a model of Christian asceticism and doctrinal orthodoxy. His writings are often used in retreats and spiritual talks, helping to deepen the spiritual life of participants.

Conclusion

T his exploration of St. Silouan the Athonite's life and teachings offers a comprehensive look at a figure whose spiritual depth and insights continue to resonate across cultures and faith traditions. Through detailed examinations of his humble beginnings, profound spiritual experiences, and the core principles of his teachings, this book highlights how St. Silouan's messages of humility, prayer, love, and hope in the face of despair are not only foundational elements of Orthodox Christian spirituality but also universally applicable wisdom that speaks to the human condition in modern times.

St. Silouan's approach to combating despair and fostering a deep connection with God through the Jesus Prayer provides a valuable framework for anyone grappling with the complexities and challenges of contemporary life. His emphasis on humility as the bedrock of spiritual growth, and his teachings on the transformative power of divine love, offer guidance and solace to those seeking spiritual depth and a more meaningful engagement with their faith and community.

The global impact of St. Silouan, evidenced by his canonization and the widespread veneration of his life and work, underscores his significance not just as a religious figure but as a beacon of spiritual wisdom. His influence extends beyond the confines of monastic life, touching the lives of laypeople around the world and inspiring a wide array of individuals to incorporate his teachings into their daily practices and understanding of mental health.

In conclusion, St. Silouan the Athonite stands as a towering example of how profound faith and relentless pursuit of spiritual communion with God can illuminate the path for others. His legacy, as explored in this book, serves as both a guide and a source of inspiration for navigating the spiritual and existential challenges of the 21st century. By delving into his life story and teachings, readers are invited to reflect on their own spiritual journeys and are offered practical tools for fostering their own well-being and spiritual growth, rooted in the timeless wisdom of a saint who lived a life of deep prayer, humility, and love.